A TEEN GUIDE to Creative, Delightful DINNERS

by Dana Meachen Rau

CONTENT ADVISER: Joan Bushman, RD, MPH,
Dietician and Wellness Specialist

READING ADVISER: Alexa L. Sandmann, EdD, Professor of Literacy,
College and Graduate School of Education, Health, and Human Services,
Kent State University

COMPASS POINT BOOKS
a capstone imprint

Compass Point Books
151 Good Counsel Drive
P.O. Box 669
Mankato, MN 56002-0669

Editor: Jennifer Fretland VanVoorst
Designers: Veronica Correia and Heidi Thompson
Media Researcher: Wanda Winch
Food Stylist: Sarah Schuette
Library Consultant: Kathleen Baxter
Production Specialist: Sarah Bennett

Image Credits

ArtParts Stock Illustrations, illustrations of food and kitchen objects throughout book; Capstone Studio: Karon Dubke, cover
(top all), 15, 17, 19, 21, 23 (all), 25, 27, 29, 31, 33, 34 (all), 37, 39, 41, 43, 47, 49, 51, 53; Dana Meachen Rau, 64 (middle);
Getty Images Inc: Upper Cut Images/Michelle Pedone, 4–5; iStockphoto: fatihhoca, 62, Kemal Bas, 63, Neustockimages,
6-7, Stephan Hoerold, 59, akva, 8; Shutterstock: Apollofoto, cover (bottom middle right), CandyBoxPhoto, 22, Christopher
Halloran, cover (bottom right), Elke Dennis, 60, Edyta Pawlowska, 1, Elena Schweitzer, 54 (top), erwinova, 9, Ian O'Hanlon,
100% stamp used throughout book, Maksim Shmeljov, 58–59 (bottom), 62–63 (bottom), 64 (bottom), Mazzzur, cover
background, Monkey Business Images, 44–45, mypokcik, 35, Peter Baxter, 12–13, Robert Kneschke, cover (bottom middle
left), Serhiy Shullye, back cover, Thaiview, 10–11 background, Tyler Olson, cover (bottom left).

Library of Congress Cataloging-in-Publication Data
Rau, Dana Meachen, 1971–
  A Teen guide to creative, delightful dinners / by Dana Meachen Rau.
    p. cm. — (Teen cookbooks)
    title: Creative, delightful dinners
  Includes index.
  Summary: "Information and recipes help readers create quick, healthy,
and tasty dinners"—Provided by publisher.
  ISBN 978-0-7565-4408-9 (library binding)
  1. Dinners and dining—Juvenile literature. 2. Cookbooks. I. Title.
II. Title: Creative, delightful dinners.
  TX737.R28 2011
  641.5'4—dc22   2010040682

Visit Compass Point Books on the Internet at *www.capstonepub.com*

Printed in the United States of America in Stevens Point, Wisconsin.
082011   006349R

TABLE OF CONTENTS

A NIGHT ON PARTY ISLAND

Your days are probably packed. First there's the long school day. Then after-school clubs and sports or band practice or a job. And don't forget homework (although you may want to). Checking e-mail. Watching a show. Reading a book. So much to do, and so little time!

You need a break. Think of dinner as a sunny island in the middle of a stormy sea. This island isn't deserted, and it doesn't have annoying monkeys or lack food and water. This island is an oasis where you can just sit back and relax. It's a place for you to decompress from a busy day, fuel up for evening activities, and, most important, visit with family and friends.

In fact, why not make dinner into a party? The more the merrier! If you have a large family, dinner might always feel like a party. Use the time spent cooking with them to catch up on the day. If you have a small family, or if it's just you and Mom or Dad or another adult for dinner, take the chance to have a quiet evening of your own.

On nights when you aren't running in a hundred directions and you have more time, invite some friends. Parties can be a lot of work, but your friends can help prepare the meal with you. Everyone might bring a different talent to the "table." Maybe Joe's origami skills make him the perfect person to fold napkins. If Sue is good at stirring up trouble, get her to stir the soup.

Buying food for a large group can be expensive, but your friends can help with that too. Make dinner potluck—each person brings a dish. Or assign everyone ingredients to contribute, and then make dinner together.

Then sit back, relax, and enjoy your stay on party island. Take a vacation from the chaos of your day.

Party preparation starts a week or so before the big event. Before you can shop for ingredients, you need to know how many guests you'll be hosting. So once you know who's coming, make a plan and head to the store.

Produce

The produce section has all of the fruits and vegetables you'll need. Fresh is best. If you are going to eat your fruit within a day, buy it ripe. But if it's going to sit for a few days before you use it, look for fruit that's firm and a little unripe. Don't buy fruit with bruises or brown spots. Vegetables should be bright, colorful, and free of blemishes. Leafy greens, like lettuce, should look crisp, not limp or slimy.

You can get the freshest produce at a farm stand or farmers market. Some farms even invite you to visit and pick your own. Look for apple orchards or blueberry and strawberry farms where you can bring your own baskets and pay for what you pick.

Refrigerated and Frozen Foods

That's the area of the grocery store where you usually wish you were wearing a sweater. Frozen foods are kept in the aisle or aisles lined with freezer doors. Refrigerated foods are kept cold on special shelves. Here's where you'll find dairy foods, meats, poultry, fish, eggs, and other perishable items. All these foods are marked with a "use by" date. After this date, the food is likely to spoil, and eating it can make you sick. Never eat expired food.

Packaged Foods

Making everything from scratch is the best way to know something's fresh. But packaged foods can make cooking faster and easier. Read the nutrition labels of food packed in boxes, bags, cans, and cartons to see how much fat, calories, sugar, and salt they contain. Also notice the "best if used by" date on the package. After this date, the food might lose its flavor, get stale, or be unsafe to eat.

Organic Foods

The word *organic* refers to the way a food has been farmed or raised. Organic farmers don't use harmful pesticides to kill insects or chemical fertilizers to kill weeds. They use natural methods to grow produce. Organic meats are not injected with any hormones or antibiotics. You can find organic foods in many grocery stores. If you live in a rural area, seek out organic farms, not only for produce and meat, but for eggs, syrup, and jam too. If you live in a city, you might be able to visit a farmers market, where farmers bring their food from the country.

If you can, buy foods produced near your home. Why buy an apple that has been shipped thousands of miles to your grocery store when you can buy one that grew just a short distance away? By buying locally, you support your community and help the planet too.

... UpseTTing The Grownups.

Preparing for a party is a big task. In your creative cooking frenzy, the kitchen can get quite messy. Keep the kitchen as clean as you can while you cook. You'll have less cleanup at the end. The last thing you want to do after a party is stay up late washing dishes.

Put used tools in the sink and ingredients back in the cabinet or refrigerator. Wipe the counters, wash the dishes (or put them in the dishwasher), and try to leave the kitchen the same way you found it. If you really want to please the grownups, leave it even cleaner than you found it. Then they'll be more likely to help you with some of the more unpleasant jobs of cooking and cleanup, like slicing onions or scraping the broiling pan.

... Burning The House Down.

Remember when you were just a kid and you weren't allowed near the hot stove or grill? Now that you're the chef, you can finally enter the forbidden zone. But you have to be careful and alert. The flame on a gas stove or gas grill, or even the heat from an electric burner, can ignite a piece of cloth in an instant. Keep clothing, aprons, and towels away from the heat so you don't start a fire.

Even if you are careful, be prepared just in case. Keep a fire extinguisher in the kitchen. Be sure to turn off the burner on the stove or the gas on the grill when you're done. Never leave the kitchen if you're heating oil, which can easily start a fire if left unattended.

... A Trip To The Emergency Room.

Flames and hot electric burners are not the only things that can burn you. So can steam, hot liquids, and oven racks. Open the lid of a pot on the stove away from you so you don't get a sudden burst of steam in your face. Keep the handles of pots turned toward the back of the stove. If they hang over the edge, the pot can get knocked off and spill its contents all over you. Wear oven mitts whenever you are taking a pan in or out of the oven.

Be careful of sharp knives. Always watch while you cut, and cut away from you. Use sharp knives, not dull ones that can slip off the surface of food and onto your finger.

Be aware of electricity in your work space. If you use a plug-in appliance, make sure there are no puddles nearby. Don't stretch a cord across an area where people may walk. And never poke a metal object into an appliance that's plugged in.

... Seeing Your Dinner Come Back Again.

Drinking spoiled milk, eating unwashed vegetables, biting into an undercooked burger— all these can lead to one result: getting sick. If you serve these foods at a party, your guests will never want to come back!

Bacteria are the cause of food-related sickness. Bacteria are found in raw meat, poultry, fish, and eggs. Cooking these foods thoroughly at high temperatures kills the bacteria. Storing foods in the refrigerator also keeps bacteria under control. The foods will eventually spoil, but the low temperature slows bacteria's growth.

Keeping things clean is another weapon against bacteria. Start your cooking session by washing your hands with warm, soapy water. Gently rub fruits and vegetables under cold running water to remove bacteria too. If you use a knife and cutting board to cut raw meat, fish, or poultry, don't use the knife or board for anything else until they've been washed well in hot, soapy water. The high temperature of a dishwasher cleans them best. You can even use separate knives and cutting boards for meat and vegetables to be sure.

HOW TO USE THIS BOOK

This book is divided into four party menus, including main dishes, side dishes, drinks, and desserts. See how many servings each recipe makes. If you invite more friends than there are servings, you may need to double, triple, or even quadruple the recipe. But don't wait for a party to try these recipes. Sample something from each party menu to jazz up your regular dinners.

Each recipe has three lists. Food Stuff includes all the ingredients for the recipe. Kitchen Gear lets you know what tools you'll need. Prep Steps take you through the instructions to create your delicious dinner. Some cooking methods and kitchen tools may be new to you. Look them up in the back of the book in the Technique Glossary (page 58) or the Tools Glossary (page 56).

Conversion Charts

WEIGHT

UNITED STATES	METRIC
1 ounce	30 grams
½ pound	225 g
1 pound	455 g

TEMPERATURE

DEGREES FAHRENHEIT	DEGREES CELSIUS
250°F	120°C
300°F	150°C
350°F	180°C
375°F	190°C
400°F	200°C
425°F	220°C

Look for special stamps on some recipes:

Easy to Enormasize points out recipes that are simple to adjust to feed a crowd. You'll make some foods when guests are there, and others a few hours before they arrive.

Check out the *If You're a Vegetarian* stamp. Here you'll find foods to replace the nonvegetarian items in the Food Stuff lists.

The *Make Ahead* stamp will tell you which recipes, or parts of recipes, you can make a day or a few days before the party. The more you can do ahead of time, the better.

Even if you're not a vegetarian, you still may want to change a recipe. Look for the *Call in the Subs* stamp to find out about alternative ingredients.

VOLUME	UNITED STATES	METRIC
	¼ teaspoon	1 milliliter
	½ teaspoon	2.5 mL
	1 teaspoon	5 mL
	1 tablespoon	15 mL
	¼ cup	60 mL
	⅓ cup	80 mL
	½ cup	120 mL
	1 cup	250 mL
	1 quart	1 liter

KEEP AN EYE ON THE CLOCK. THE GUESTS ARE ARRIVING SOON. COLLECT YOUR INGREDIENTS AND GET COOKING!

GRILL AND CHILL: A BACKYARD BARBECUE

A backyard barbecue comes with its own set of problems. The dog's curious nose may find the chip bowl, a volleyball may crash into the dip, and the mosquitoes might eat you alive.

But for a chance for fresh air, sunshine, and good company, a meal in the great outdoors is worth every bug bite!

RIDE-THE-WAVES LEMONADE

Did you know the bright light from the sun is made up of all the colors of the rainbow? The waves travel millions of miles from the sun to your eyes. Ride the waves and try a sunny lemonade that comes in rainbow colors too.

Food Stuff

1 cup sugar

1 cup boiling water

1 cup thawed frozen raspberries or fresh raspberries

¾ cup lemon juice

Cold water

Ice

1 lemon

Kitchen Gear

Liquid measuring cup

Glass mixing bowl

Spoon

Blender

Makes four to six servings

Sweet or Tart?

Berries are naturally sweet, so along with the sugar, they add sweetness to your lemonade. If you like tart lemonade that makes your lips curl, reduce the amount of sugar in the recipe.

Prep Steps

1. Combine the sugar and boiling water in a glass bowl. Mix until the sugar dissolves and the water looks clear with no grains of sugar. Let cool.

2. Puree the raspberries in the blender. If necessary, add a tablespoon or two of cold water so the mixture is liquid with no chunks. Add the fruit to the sugar water.

3. Add the lemon juice to the other liquids. Stir well.

4. Pour ½ cup of the fruit and sugar mixture into a glass. Add 1 cup of cold water. Stir well.

5. Add ice. Slice the lemon into ¼-inch (0.6-centimeter) slices. Hook a slice onto the side of the glass.

6. Repeat with more glasses.

Call in the Sub

To get an array of rainbow colors, substitute the raspberries with these other fruits:

Red: cherries

Orange: peach nectar

Yellow: grapefruit juice

Green: lime and mint (You may need to add some extra sugar, because lime juice isn't sweet. Garnish with mint leaves.)

Blue: blueberries

Purple: blackberries

Fresh Juice

If you have a juicer, you can easily squeeze the juice from fresh lemons. To get a cup of juice, you'll need about five or six lemons. You can also squeeze the juice by hand.

Make Ahead

Instead of making the lemonade by the glass, make a whole pitcher and keep it in the fridge until guests arrive.

STRAWBERRY SUMMER SALAD

Nothing says summer like a plump red strawberry. OK, a strawberry doesn't really talk—but what if it did? It might tell you when it's ripe. It might yelp when you cut off its stem. It might suggest that you add it to a tossed salad!

Food Stuff

6 cups loosely packed salad greens

8 to 10 strawberries

½ cup chopped walnuts

¼ cup olive oil

2 tablespoons balsamic vinegar

1 tablespoon sugar

2.5 ounces goat cheese, crumbled

Serves four

Kitchen Gear

Liquid measuring cup

Dry measuring cups

Measuring spoons

Salad bowl

Knife

Small mixing bowl

Whisk

Salad tongs

Prep Steps

1. Wash the salad greens (if not prewashed), dry, and place in a large salad bowl.

2. Cut each strawberry into quarters. Add to the greens.

3. Add the walnuts.

4. In a separate small bowl, beat the oil, vinegar, and sugar with the whisk until the liquids are no longer transparent.

5. Pour over the greens. Toss until well coated with dressing.

6. Sprinkle goat cheese on each serving.

Call in the Subs

Cheese and fruit make a nice combination in salads. Besides strawberries and goat cheese, try pairing blueberries and cheddar, or dried cranberries and blue cheese.

HOME RUN SLIDERS

Bases loaded, two outs, and you're up at bat. Your brow is sweating, your knees are knocking, and your hands are shaking. You feel the pressure to hit a home run.

Hit a home run every time with these mini buffalo-style burgers. Unlike the big game, these meaty bites won't stress you out.

Food Stuff

1 pound lean ground turkey

1½ teaspoons hot pepper sauce

2 teaspoons honey

1 teaspoon red wine vinegar

½ teaspoon smoked paprika

½ teaspoon black pepper

3 tablespoons plain bread crumbs

Vegetable cooking spray

2 stalks celery, cut into thin strips

Light blue cheese dressing

8 to 10 round whole grain dinner rolls, sliced in half

Kitchen Gear

Measuring spoons

Knife

Mixing bowl

Gas grill

Turner

Makes eight 2-ounce sliders

Keep IT Clean!

It's easiest to mix the meat and form the patties with your hands. After you're done, be sure to wash your hands with warm, soapy water. You can get sick from uncooked meat, and your eyes can sting if you touch them after handling hot sauce.

Prep Steps

1. Place the ground turkey in a mixing bowl. Add the hot sauce, honey, vinegar, paprika, pepper, and bread crumbs.

2. Mix well with your hands. Form into eight flat, round patties, about 2 ounces each.

3. Spray the grates of the gas grill with cooking spray.

4. Heat the grill on high for about five minutes.

5. Lay the patties on the grill. Cook on medium heat for five minutes. Flip over with a turner. Cook about five more minutes on the other side or until the centers are well done.

6. Take the patties off the grill with a turner. Place them on the bottoms of the dinner rolls. Pour about 1 tablespoon of dressing on top of each burger. Add a few strips of celery. Top with the upper half of the roll.

If You're a Vegetarian

If you don't eat turkey, beef, or chicken, try a veggie burger. You can find them in your grocer's freezer. Make sure you buy unseasoned ones so the sauce doesn't clash. Or you can try grilling a Portobello mushroom cap. These large mushrooms are meaty alternatives to burgers. Brush them with the mixture of hot sauce, honey, vinegar, paprika, and pepper before grilling.

Call in the Subs

You can use ground beef or ground chicken for this recipe too.

Grill Safety

Have an adult show you how to use a gas grill. It's important to scrape the racks clean before cooking, watch out for the open flame, and turn off the gas when you are done.

Make Ahead

Make the patties ahead of time and keep them in the fridge. Cook them at dinnertime so guests can enjoy them hot off the grill.

SORBET SANDWICHES

I scream, you scream, we all scream for ... sorbet! It is a fruity alternative to ice cream, and sorbet fits just as well between two cookies to make an easy-to-eat treat.

Food Stuff

1 quart fruit sorbet
   (any flavor)
20 vanilla wafer cookies
Rainbow sprinkles

Kitchen Gear

Small plate
Tablespoon
Baking sheet

Makes 10 sandwiches

Prep Steps

1. Pour the sprinkles onto a small plate.

2. Place a rounded tablespoon of sorbet on one cookie. Place another cookie on top. Squeeze slightly so the sorbet starts poking out the sides.

3. Roll the edges of the sorbet in the sprinkles. Set aside on a baking sheet.

4. Repeat with the rest of the cookies.

5. Place the baking sheet in the freezer. Freeze the cookie sandwiches for at least a half an hour before eating.

Frozen Fruit

Ice cream is the ultimate summer treat. But it's made with real cream, and has a lot of fat and calories. Sorbet does not contain any dairy products. It's made from pureed fruit, sugar, and water.

Make Ahead

You can easily make these the day before your party. Once they have become firm in the freezer, place them in an airtight container and keep them in the freezer until it's time for dessert.

Call in the Subs

Instead of rolling sprinkles around the edges, try flaked coconut, mini chocolate chips, or granola.

CIAO, CHOW!
AN ITALIAN FEAST

You have to fly over the Mediterranean to see Italy's unique boot shape. You have to visit the canals of Venice to ride in a gondola. You have to vacation in Rome to behold the ruins of the Coliseum. But you don't even have to leave home to get the great taste of Italian cooking. Invite friends over for a feast of fresh ingredients.

ANTIPASTO SKEWERS

If you're going to serve an Italian feast, you need to learn a little Italian. Antipasto means "before the meal." In English, it means appetizers. It's traditionally served as a first course and contains almost any item found in Italian kitchens, such as meats, cheeses, and marinated vegetables. The colors in this antipasto are the same as those in the Italian flag: red, white, and green. So wave your skewer proudly and enjoy these pre-dinner bites.

Food Stuff

16 grape tomatoes

16 tiny balls of fresh mozzarella

1 can marinated artichoke hearts

16 slices turkey pepperoni

16 pitted black olives

16 Spanish Manzanilla olives stuffed with pimientos

Kitchen Gear

Wooden *skewers*

Makes eight skewers

Prep Steps

1. Onto each skewer, slide two of each of the ingredients. Arrange them in any order you like.

2. Line them up on a platter to serve. Guests can either eat right off the skewer (be careful of the pointy end!) or push the pieces off the skewer onto a plate with their forks.

If You're a Vegetarian

With so many other flavors to choose from, you can easily leave meat off these skewers.

Call in the Subs

Antipasto can be any combination of Italian cheese, meats, and vegetables that you like. Try provolone or Parmesan cheese instead of mozzarella. Check out the deli for Italian meats, such as prosciutto, salami, or cappicola. Anchovies, a type of fish packed in oil, are a good choice. Marinated eggplant or sweet or hot peppers are nice additions too.

GARLIC BREAD NACHOS

What's your favorite part of a big plate of nachos? The stringy cheese, the spicy flavor, or the dipping sauce? Put a new spin on this ultimate group appetizer by combining the fun of nachos with the bold taste of garlic bread.

Food Stuff

1 6-ounce bag of salted bagel chips

1 cup grated mozzarella cheese

¾ teaspoon garlic powder

1½ teaspoons dried parsley

1 cup Super Simple Sauce (p. 28) for dipping

Kitchen Gear

Dry measuring cups

Measuring spoons

Mixing bowl

Plate

Microwave

Serves four to six

Prep Steps

1. In a mixing bowl, place the cheese, garlic powder, and parsley. Toss together until well-mixed.

2. On a large flat plate, place about half of the bagel chips.

3. Sprinkle on about half of the cheese mixture.

4. Layer on the rest of the bagel chips, and sprinkle on the rest of the cheese.

5. Microwave on high for about one minute or more, until the cheese melts.

6. Serve with the sauce for dipping.

Make It a Meal

Garlic bread nachos are a great accompaniment to an Italian dinner, but with a few additions, they can be hearty enough to be a meal in and of themselves. Try adding Italian ingredients such as pepperoni, Italian sausage, artichoke hearts, chopped tomatoes, or black or green olives. Put them on between the layers of cheese to melt them to the chips.

SUPER SIMPLE SAUCE

One basic skill every Italian chef needs is the ability to make a good tomato sauce. It's even better when that skill is super simple to learn.

Food Stuff

1 tablespoon olive oil

2 cloves garlic

½ cup onion, chopped

1 14.5-ounce can diced tomatoes

1 28-ounce can crushed tomatoes

1 6-ounce can tomato paste

1 tablespoon dried basil

Kitchen Gear

Dry measuring cups

Measuring spoons

Can opener

6-quart stockpot

Cutting board

Chef's knife

Spoon

Makes about 6 cups of sauce

Prep Steps

1. Pour the olive oil into the stockpot and place it on the stove. Heat the oil on medium high.

2. On a cutting board, chop the onion and mince the garlic. Add the onion and garlic to the oil in the pot. Stir and cook for about four minutes until the onion starts to brown and turns a little transparent.

3. Add the diced tomatoes, crushed tomatoes, tomato paste, and basil. Stir well.

4. Bring the sauce to a boil. Then reduce heat to low. Cover the pot and simmer the sauce for about 30 minutes, stirring occasionally.

Easy to Enormasize

Increase the amounts above to make enough sauce to last for a few meals. You can freeze sauce in airtight containers.

How To Chop an Onion

Cut off the top and bottom of the onion and peel away the papery skin. Cut the onion in half lengthwise from top to bottom. Place one half flat on the cutting board. Cut the onion in about five slices. Then turn it and cut five slices the other way. Because an onion grows in layers, it should break apart into many little pieces.

How To
Mince Garlic

Place a clove of garlic, skin and all, on the cutting board. Place the flat side of the chef's knife over the clove. Carefully press down on the flat side of the knife with your hand to crush the garlic. The papery skin should now easily peel off the garlic. Then rock the blade of the knife back and forth over the garlic to cut it into tiny pieces.

Make Ahead

You'll definitely want to make your sauce earlier in the day. You can reheat it on the stove before you serve it.

LOTS OF LAYERS LASAGNA

What's your favorite Italian meal? Pasta or pizza? Get the taste of both with this many-layered lasagna that combines noodles, cheese, and meat in one pan.

Food Stuff

9 whole wheat lasagna noodles

1 tablespoon olive oil

8 ounces hot Italian sausage

1 15-ounce container part-skim ricotta cheese

1 cup mozzarella cheese, grated

¼ cup Parmesan cheese, grated

Salt and pepper

Another ½ cup mozzarella cheese, grated

Super Simple Sauce (p. 28)

Kitchen Gear

Dry measuring cups

6-quart stockpot

Colander

Paper towels

Large skillet

Spoon

Plate

Spreader

12- x 7½- x 2-inch (30- x 19- x 5-cm) baking pan

Makes six to eight servings

Prep Steps

1. Prepare recipe for Super Simple Sauce (p. 28).

2. Preheat oven to 350°F.

3. Cook the noodles in a stockpot according to package directions. Drain the noodles in a colander, rinse with cold water, lay on paper towels, and pat dry.

4. Pour the olive oil into a skillet and heat on medium high on the stove. Add the sausage. Cook it for five to seven minutes, breaking it up with a spoon, until the sausage is brown and crumbly. Place the sausage on a plate covered with paper towels. The paper towels will soak up any extra fat.

5. In a mixing bowl, combine the ricotta, mozzarella, and Parmesan. Add salt and pepper to taste.

6. Divide the cheese mixture among the lasagna noodles, and spread the cheese mixture onto each one, as if you were buttering pieces of bread.

7. To assemble the lasagna, spoon some sauce into the bottom of the baking dish. Lay three noodles lengthwise in the pan, cheese side up, to cover the bottom. Sprinkle half of the sausage over the noodles. Add more sauce.

8. Layer on three more noodles, sprinkle on the rest of the sausage, and add more sauce.

9. Lay on the final three noodles. Pour on the rest of the sauce. Sprinkle another ½ cup of mozzarella on top.

10. Cover the baking dish with foil. Bake in the oven, covered, at 350°F for about 45 minutes, or until the sauce starts to bubble.

If You're a Vegetarian

Omit the sausage. You can add extra flavor to lasagna with many varieties of vegetables. Try grilled vegetables, such as eggplant, zucchini, and peppers. Cook mushrooms or spinach in a little olive oil in a skillet and add as a layer to the lasagna.

Make Ahead

Assemble your lasagna early in the day. Keep it in the fridge until close to dinnertime. But don't move the pan right from the fridge into a hot oven. Either take it out ahead of time to let it reach room temperature or place the lasagna in the oven while you preheat it to gradually bring the cold pan to cooking temperature.

LEANING TOWER OF PIZZELLES

The leaning tower in the Italian town of Pisa looks as if it is about to topple onto tourists below. It is actually the bell tower of a nearby cathedral. Many tourists take pictures of each other pretending to hold up the slanting structure.

Keep this tower of cookies and cream from crashing over by eating it up!

Food Stuff

1 cup part-skim ricotta cheese

$\frac{1}{3}$ cup confectioner's sugar

$\frac{1}{4}$ teaspoon vanilla

$\frac{1}{4}$ cup mini chocolate chips

12 Italian pizzelle cookies (or other thin cookies)

Kitchen Gear

Dry measuring cups

Measuring spoons

Electric hand mixer

Spatula

Makes two towers

Prep Steps

1. Place the ricotta, sugar, and vanilla in a mixing bowl. Blend with an electric hand mixer for about a minute until smooth. Scrape the sides with a spatula.

2. Spread about 1½ tablespoons of the cream mixture onto a pizzelle cookie. Top with another cookie. Repeat with four more pizzelles. Then begin a new tower.

3. Serve the cookies stacked on top of each other in a tall tower.

Easy to Enormasize

Just mix up more cream, and you'll have enough for a whole package of pizzelles. But don't make the tower too high! You don't want the leaning tower to become a sloppy mess on the floor!

Make Ahead

Make the cream ahead of time, but wait to assemble until you are ready to serve so the cookies don't get soggy.

ToTaLLy TubuLar

Cannoli are a popular tube-shaped Italian pastry. They're usually filled with this delicious cream mixture. Give them a try!

COZY COMFORT:

A COLD-WEATHER MENU

Are you cold to the bone after a day of skiing, tubing, snowboarding, skating, or working outside? Are you chilled to the core after a shivery stroll home in the rain? Come inside and cozy up to food that will warm you inside and out.

HOME SWEET HOME CIDER

Hot apple cider simmering on the stove is like a welcome mat for your nose. When your guests arrive, the sweet smell of this bubbling beverage will instantly make them feel at home.

Food Stuff

5 cups apple cider

2 cups pomegranate blueberry juice

2 teaspoons almond extract

1 teaspoon cinnamon

½ teaspoon cloves

½ teaspoon nutmeg

Kitchen Gear

Liquid measuring cup

Measuring spoons

Stockpot

Spoon

Mugs

Ladle

Serves six to eight

Prep Steps

1. Pour the cider and juice into the stockpot. Add the almond extract, cinnamon, cloves, and nutmeg. Stir well.

2. Heat covered on high until the liquid boils. Turn down to low and simmer covered for 30 minutes.

3. Strain the liquid through a strainer into a large glass bowl. Rinse the pot to remove the solids, and return the cider to the pot.

4. Place the pot back on the stove and simmer on low. Serve right from the pot, filling mugs with a ladle.

Easy to Enormasize

Increase the amount of ingredients to make more cider, as long as you have a pot that will fit it all!

Make Ahead

Get this brew going before your guests arrive so the sweet smell greets them at the door.

Pomegranate Power

Pomegranates are a very healthful fruit, packed with vitamin C. Some people like to eat the red, drippy seeds. Try them on salads and mixed in yogurt, or pop them into your mouth like popcorn.

MOSH PIT SOUP

A mosh pit can get dangerous with crazy dancers crashing into each other. But veggies feel no pain. This soup has room for anything you want to toss in. Build the base of the soup, and then assign an ingredient to each person coming to your party. Add their contributions as they arrive, and soon you'll have a bubbling pot of vegetables crashing into each other—but safely confined to your stove!

Food Stuff

2 tablespoons olive oil, divided

¾ pound lean ground beef

2 cloves garlic, minced

1 cup chopped onion

1 cup chopped celery

1 cup peeled and chopped carrot

1 cup frozen corn

1 cup peeled and chopped zucchini

1 cup green beans, cut into bite-sized pieces

2 unpeeled washed potatoes, diced

1 14.5-ounce can diced tomatoes

2 cups beef broth

4 cups vegetable broth

1 teaspoon salt

¼ teaspoon pepper

Kitchen Gear

Liquid measuring cup

Dry measuring cups

Measuring spoons

Large skillet

Spoon

6-quart stockpot

Knife

Cutting board

Ladle

Serves six to eight

Easy to Enormasize

If you find you have more veggies than your broth can handle, just add more broth to increase the number of people this soup can serve.

Prep Steps

1. Heat 1 tablespoon of the olive oil in a skillet. Add the ground beef. Cook and stir the beef until browned, about five to six minutes. Drain off oil if necessary. Set aside.

2. Heat the other tablespoon of olive oil in a stockpot on medium high. Cook the garlic and onion for about six minutes or until the onion starts to brown.

3. Add the celery, carrot, corn, zucchini, green beans, potatoes, and tomatoes.

4. Pour in the beef and vegetable broths. Add the cooked ground beef and the salt and pepper. Stir well.

5. Cover and heat on high until boiling. Then turn down the heat to medium low and simmer covered for 45 minutes, stirring occasionally.

6. Ladle into bowls and serve.

Call in the Subs

Any vegetable you can imagine can become a part of this soup. Try sweet potatoes or butternut squash. Toss in some spinach, kale, or Swiss chard. Why not peas, lima beans, or edamame?

If You're a Vegetarian

Replace the 2 cups of beef broth with more vegetable broth. Omit the ground beef. Instead, add 2 cups of red kidney beans, drained and rinsed, in the last 10 minutes of cooking.

The More, The Merrier

Just as it's nice to have a variety of people at your party, it's nice to have a variety of vegetables in your soup. Take this chance to try some veggies you've never tried before!

MASHED POTATO SUNDAES

Who says sundaes are for dessert? You can make sundaes out of mashed potatoes and a variety of tasty toppings. Guests will appreciate the freedom to make their own unique creations.

Food Stuff

- 3 pounds all-purpose potatoes
- 2 cups chicken broth
- 2 tablespoons butter
- 3 tablespoons skim milk
- Salt and pepper to taste
- Toppings (see list below)

Kitchen Gear

- Vegetable peeler
- Knife
- Stockpot
- Fork
- Potato masher
- Stemmed glasses

Serves six

Easy to Enormasize

Just boil up more potatoes and put out more toppings.

Prep Steps

1. Peel and rinse the potatoes. Cut out any dark spots.

2. Cut the potatoes into large chunks. Place in the stockpot. Pour in the broth. Add water to the pot until the liquid covers the potatoes.

3. Cook covered over high heat until the liquid starts to boil. Then turn heat to low and simmer for about 20 to 30 minutes or until the potatoes are very soft when pierced with a fork.

4. Take the pot off the heat. Use a colander to carefully drain the water into the sink. Put the potatoes back in the pot. Add the butter and milk to the potatoes. Mash them with a potato masher until smooth.

5. To serve, place about 1 cup of mashed potatoes in a glass. Dress up your naked potatoes with any of these toppings:

   Sauces: sour cream, salsa, chili, gravy

   Cheeses: grated cheddar, crumbled Gorgonzola, grated Monterey jack

   Veggies: cooked broccoli, chives, cooked onions, jalapeños, diced avocado, red or green peppers, peas, corn

   Meat/Beans: crumbled bacon, diced ham, black beans, red kidney beans

Make Ahead

You can make the potatoes ahead of time. Store the mashed potatoes in a casserole dish. Before it's time to eat, you can reheat the potatoes in the oven or the microwave. You can also prepare all of your topping bowls before the party. Keep them in the fridge until ready to serve.

COMPOST THe PeeLS!

Composting is a great way to reduce the trash in a landfill and help your outdoor garden at the same time. Toss natural trash from fruits and vegetables, such as potato peels, in your garden. Rake them into the dirt. They will slowly decompose and turn into nutrient-rich soil.

If You're a Vegetarian

Use all water instead of chicken broth to boil your potatoes. Avoid the meat toppings and fill up on a variety of vegetables!

41

WELL-FED GINGERBREAD SHORTCAKES

Gingerbread men are little, flat, crispy people-shaped cookies. Try this well-fed gingerbread—it's bigger, puffier, and softer. Serve it warm for a cozy end to your cold-weather meal.

Food Stuff

2 cups baking mix

3 tablespoons packed brown sugar

⅓ cup molasses

2 tablespoons melted butter

⅓ cup plain nonfat yogurt

1½ teaspoons ginger

1 teaspoon cinnamon

¼ teaspoon allspice

2 fresh pears

6 ounces fresh blackberries

1 6-ounce container nonfat lemon yogurt

Kitchen Gear

Dry measuring cups

Measuring spoons

Mixing bowls

Spatula

Baking sheet

Knife

Spoon

Serves six

Prep Steps

1. Preheat oven to 400°F.

2. In a mixing bowl, combine the baking mix, sugar, molasses, butter, yogurt, ginger, cinnamon, and allspice. Stir with a rubber spatula until the ingredients form a ball of dough.

3. Place the dough on a flat surface sprinkled with baking mix. Knead the dough about five times.

4. Divide the dough into six equal balls. Flatten the balls into discs and place them on an ungreased baking sheet.

5. Bake at 400°F for 10 to 12 minutes.

6. Core the pears and cut them into small chunks. Rinse the blackberries. Place the fruits in a bowl. Add the yogurt and stir gently.

7. Serve the shortcake by placing it on a plate with a spoonful of yogurt and fruit mixture on top.

Make Ahead

If you can't time these shortcakes to be hot out of the oven at dessert time, make them beforehand and heat them for about 15 seconds in the microwave before serving.

PARTY WITH A PURPOSE

The world would be boring if everyone looked and acted the same. We're lucky to live among people with many personalities and opinions. As citizens of the world, we have a lot in common. Yet we have differences too.

A party is a great way to get a group together and listen to everyone's ideas. You can use the opportunity to raise awareness for a cause and share thoughts for making the world a better place for everyone.

STOP-GLOBAL-WARMING PUNCH

Those poor polar bears! We need to think about ways to stop climate change so their icy habitat stops shrinking. Remind your guests of the polar bears' plight with this tasty punch, complete with a melting ice floe.

Food Stuff

- 1 64-ounce bottle white grape juice
- 1 quart ginger ale
- 16 ounces blue raspberry juice

Kitchen Gear

- Liquid measuring cup
- Tube pan
- Large punch bowl
- Ladle
- Plastic polar bears

Makes six 8-ounce servings

Easy to Enormasize

As long as your punch bowl can fit the liquid, add as much ginger ale and blue raspberry juice as you like to satisfy your thirsty crowd. As the party progresses, you can keep adding punch to the bowl.

Prep Steps

1. To create an ice ring, pour white grape juice into the tube pan until the juice is about an inch (2.5 cm) from the top of the pan. Let the ice ring freeze overnight.

2. When it's time for the party, take the ice ring out of the freezer. Turn the pan upside down and run warm water over the bottom of the pan. Keep your hand ready to catch the ice ring when it comes loose and drops down. (Maybe someone can help you with this step.)

3. Place the ice ring in a large punch bowl.

4. Pour in the ginger ale, the blue raspberry juice, and any white grape juice left over from making the ring.

Make Ahead

The ice ring has to be made far ahead of party time. It is best to make it the day before to give it a full 24 hours to harden.

5. Place the polar bears on top of the ice ring.

6. Serve the punch into cups with a ladle.

Why Not Ice Water?

If you make your ice ring out of water, it will dilute the flavors of your punch. By making the ring out of another kind of juice, the melting ring will only add flavor to the bowl.

Call in the Subs

Any combination of fruit juices with something fizzy makes a tasty punch. Besides ginger ale, your "fizzy" can also be flavored seltzer water, lemon-lime soda, or orange soda. Pineapple, pomegranate, cherry, cranberry, and apple juices can add layers of flavor to the ice ring.

PICK-A-COLOR PIZZA

Some people see life in black and white—with two clear sides to every issue. Some see life in red—through rosy-colored glasses that always look on the bright side. Others see life in green—like a traffic light urging them to GO and see where life takes them.

Pick a color of pizza that suits you. Or mix up ingredients to make a colorful pie to reflect your unique personality.

Food Stuff

8-inch whole wheat individual pizza crust (precooked)

Olive oil

½ cup grated mozzarella cheese

For Red Pizza

2-3 strips roasted red peppers (about 1 tablespoon chopped)

¼ cup sun-dried tomatoes

3 tablespoons Super Simple Sauce (p. 28)

6 slices turkey pepperoni

For White Pizza

1 clove garlic

2 tablespoons chopped onion

½ teaspoon olive oil

2 tablespoons part-skim ricotta cheese

1 tablespoon grated Parmesan cheese

Dried rosemary

For Black Pizza

Small eggplant (about ⅓ cup cooked and chopped)

6 kalamata olives, sliced

¼ cup sliced mushrooms, washed

Olive oil

1½ tablespoons Super Simple Sauce (p. 28)

Black pepper

Kitchen Gear

Dry measuring cups

Measuring spoons

Knife

Small skillet

Broiling pan

Pastry brush

Baking sheet

Pizza Bar

Let guests make their own pizzas by putting all the toppings in bowls on a counter or table. Give each person an empty crust, and let the guests pile on whatever toppings they like.

For Green Pizza

1 cup packed uncooked baby spinach leaves

½ teaspoon olive oil

5 slices green tomato

1 tablespoon pesto sauce

48

Prep Steps

1. Preheat the oven to 425°F.

2. Prepare the toppings as follows:

   For Red Pizza: Chop the roasted red peppers with a knife. Cut the sun-dried tomatoes into thin strips.

   For White Pizza: Mince the garlic and chop the onion into small pieces. Place in a skillet with ½ teaspoon of olive oil. Cook and stir on medium high for about three to four minutes until nicely browned.

   For Black Pizza: Cut the eggplant lengthwise into ½-inch (1.3-cm) slices. Brush with olive oil. Broil on high for five minutes. Flip them over and broil for three more minutes. Remove the eggplant from the oven and chop into small pieces. Set aside. Chop the mushrooms into small pieces. Place in a skillet with ½ teaspoon of olive oil. Cook and stir on medium high for about two minutes until browned.

   For Green Pizza: Place the spinach in a skillet with olive oil. Cook and stir on medium high just until the spinach wilts. Cut the tomato into ¼-inch (0.6-cm) thick slices. Remove the seeds and pulp.

3. Place the crust on the baking sheet and brush with olive oil. Then layer toppings as follows:

   For Red Pizza: Spread crust with sauce, then add peppers, tomatoes, and pepperoni.

   For White Pizza: Spread the crust with ricotta, then add the garlic and onion mixture. Sprinkle with Parmesan and rosemary.

   For Black Pizza: Spread the crust with sauce, then add mushrooms, eggplant, olives, and black pepper.

   For Green Pizza: Spread the crust with pesto, then add the tomato slices and the spinach.

4. Top with the mozzarella cheese.

5. Bake at 425°F for about eight minutes (or according to pizza crust package directions) until the cheese is melted and slightly browned.

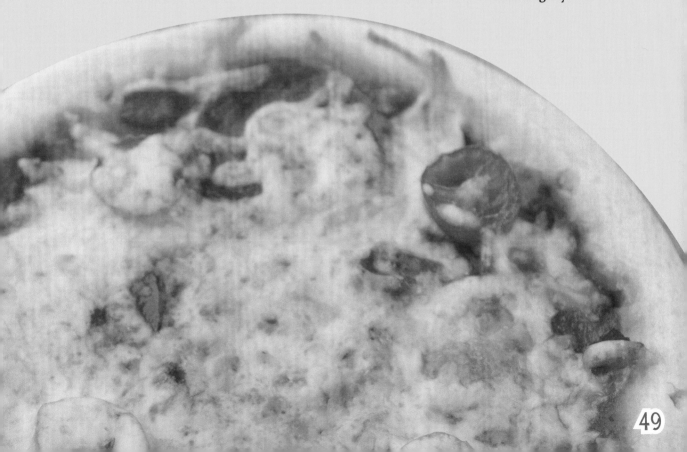

SIMPLE SOLUTION CAESAR SALAD

The world is filled with problems to solve. Some of them seem impossible. But by working together, you and your friends can get things done. The best solutions are often the simplest ones. That goes for dinnertime too! Here's the problem: You need a tasty side dish for your meal. The solution? Caesar salad! It's so easy to make you'll feel as if you can conquer the world's problems with ease.

Food Stuff

For the croutons

Four ends of whole grain bread (about 4 cups cubed)

2 tablespoons olive oil

½ teaspoon garlic powder

¼ teaspoon salt

¼ teaspoon pepper

For the salad

About 12 large leaves of romaine lettuce

½ cup freshly grated Parmesan cheese

Light Caesar dressing

Kitchen Gear

Pizza cutter

Mixing bowl

Spoon

Baking sheet

Turner

Four salad plates

Serves four

Make It Dinner

You can have Caesar Salad as your main meal by adding strips of cooked chicken on top.

Prep Steps

1. Preheat the oven to 350°F. Use a pizza cutter to cut the bread into 1-inch (2.5-cm) cubes.

2. In a mixing bowl, mix the bread cubes with olive oil, garlic powder, salt, and pepper until well coated.

3. Place the bread cubes in one layer on a baking sheet.

4. Bake at 350°F for about 15 minutes, flipping the cubes every five minutes with a turner. Take them out of the oven and let them cool.

5. Wash and dry the lettuce leaves. Place about three lettuce leaves on each plate.

6. Sprinkle Parmesan cheese and a fourth of the croutons on each salad. Pour about 1 tablespoon of dressing on top.

Make Ahead

You should make the salad fresh when you're ready to serve it. But you can make the croutons up to a day ahead of time and keep them in a zippered bag or other airtight container.

No-Waste Croutons!

Making croutons is a great way to use up the ends of loaves of bread that everyone seems to leave behind. Or you can make croutons from bread that has gone stale (make sure it isn't moldy, though!). Collect ends and stale bread, and store them in a plastic bag in the freezer until you have enough to make a batch of croutons.

MELTING POT FONDUE

The United States has been called a melting pot because immigrants from countries all over the world have combined to form the American population. Dip into this sweet mix with a melting pot of chocolate and peanut butter, and appreciate the variety of people that makes this country great.

Food Stuff

¾ cup semisweet chocolate chips

¾ cup peanut butter chips

¼ cup milk

Pretzels

Marshmallows

Bananas

Kitchen Gear

Dry measuring cups

1-quart saucepan

Wooden spoon

5-inch (13-cm) ramekin

Hot pad

Plate

Forks

Serves four to six

Prep Steps

1. Place the empty ramekin in an oven set at 250°F. Let it warm for about 10 minutes.

2. On the stovetop, heat the chips and milk in a saucepan on medium low heat for about five minutes, stirring constantly, until smooth.

3. Take the ramekin out of the oven (it will be hot, so use an oven mitt!). Pour in the fondue.

4. Place the dish on a hot pad where you'll be eating dessert.

5. Arrange the dipping items—the pretzels, marshmallows, and bananas—on a separate plate. Give everyone a fork, and dip in!

IT MUST BE MELTY

Fondue pots sit above a small container of burning fuel or a tea light candle to keep the fondue warm as you eat it. Warming the casserole dish keeps the fondue warm as well. If the fondue sits out long enough to cool and harden, you can just put the casserole dish in the microwave. Heat it for short intervals, stirring between, until the chocolate re-melts.

Call in the Subs

Isn't everything good dipped in chocolate? Other fondue dippers are cubes of pound cake, pineapple chunks, strawberries, cherries, dried apricots, or small chocolate chip cookies!

Instead of peanut butter chips, you can have an all-chocolate fondue by mixing semisweet and milk chocolate. Toss in mint chips or butterscotch chips for more unusual flavors.

A good party always has a spread of food on the table. Things to dip, things to spread, and things to sink your fork into. With all the chatter, laughter, and eating, you may be full before you know it.

But fill yourself up with the right foods. The right foods give your body energy. The wrong foods slow you down. You don't want to leave a party feeling as though you just ate a ton of bricks. The more healthful the food, the more your body will thank you at the end of the night.

CARBOHYDRATES

Lots of foods contain sugar. Not just cookies, cake, or soda, but also bread, pasta, fruit, and veggies. The sugars your body uses from food are called carbohydrates. Your body turns carbohydrates into energy to keep all of your internal systems working well. Stock up on good carbohydrates, and your body will have energy to burn.

Grains: A big bowl of pasta, a thick pizza crust, a side of rice. These foods are all made from grain. Wheat, rice, oats, and corn all contain carbohydrates. The best grains are whole grains—they're still filled with nutrients. Avoid refined grains, which have been stripped of many healthful ingredients.

Fruits and vegetables: Think of ways to put fruits and veggies on your dinner menu. A big lettuce salad with tomatoes, carrots, cucumbers, olives, and peppers will fill you up with the nutrients your body craves.

PROTEIN

Your bones, muscles, and body tissues need protein. Of all the meals and snacks of your day, dinner usually packs in the most.

Meat, poultry, fish, and eggs: A juicy steak, pork chop, chicken breast, fish filet, and cheesy omelet all have lots of protein. Look for lean cuts of meat (that means beef and pork without a lot of fat, and chicken with no skin).

Beans: Black beans, navy beans, pinto beans, soybeans, and all the other colorful varieties can replace meat in many dishes.

Nuts: Add flavor and garnish to dinners and desserts by sprinkling on protein-packed nuts.

Dairy products: Milk, cheese, and yogurt, and anything made from them, will provide you with protein as well as bone-building calcium. Look for low fat or nonfat dairy products.

FAT AND SALT

Hold the butter! Stop that shaker! Your body needs some fat and salt to function, but not too much. The fat in your body stores energy. That's why when you exercise, you're not just burning energy, but burning fat too. Salt balances the levels of the fluids in your body. But so many foods on grocery store shelves today are brimming with more fat and salt than your body needs. That makes you gain unnecessary weight, stresses out your heart, and generally slows you down.

So buy low fat foods when you can. Get your fats from fish, nuts, and plant oils (such as olive oil, vegetable oil, and sunflower oil) instead of from solid fats, such as butter, shortening, and lard. It's OK to sprinkle a little salt on your dinner, but taste your food first. Too much can hide the delicious flavors you spent so much time creating!

You only get one body. Keep it working its best with delicious, healthy dinners!

You only get one body. Keep it working its best with delicious, healthy dinners!

TOOLS GLOSSARY

Baking pan
flat metal pan with high sides for baking cakes and brownies

Baking sheet
flat metal pan used to bake cookies and other baked goods

Blender
appliance with a rotating blade that mixes solids and liquids

Chef's knife
knife with a large, wide blade

Colander
bowl dotted with holes to drain liquids from foods

Dry measuring cups
containers the size of specific standard measurements. Dry cups come in ¼ cup, ⅓ cup, ½ cup, and 1 cup sizes. Measure dry ingredients over an empty bowl, not over your mixture, in case of spills. Level off dry ingredients with a table knife.

Electric hand mixer
appliance that uses beaters to mix, blend, and whip foods

Hot pad
special mat to protect tables from hot food and spills

Ladle
tool with a bowl-shaped end for scooping liquids

Liquid measuring cup
container marked at intervals along the sides to measure accurate amounts of liquid. Liquid measuring cups are usually marked at ¼ cup, ⅓ cup, ½ cup, ⅔ cup, ¾ cup, and 1 cup intervals. Hold the measuring cup at eye level to check the measurement.

Measuring spoons
spoons the size of specific standard measurements. Measuring spoons come in ¼ teaspoon, ½ teaspoon, 1 teaspoon, and 1 tablespoon measurements. There are 3 teaspoons in a tablespoon.

Microwave
appliance that cooks food with radio waves. Make sure the cup, bowl, or plate you use is microwave-safe. Microwaving heats food and the container it's in, so use oven mitts to remove it from the microwave.

Pastry brush
small brush used to apply liquids on top of foods

Pizza cutter
tool with a wheel-shaped blade that rolls over a food to cut it

Potato masher
tool used to crush soft foods into a lumpy mixture

Ramekin
small dish for cooking or serving small amounts

Salad Tongs
tool made of two attached sides that can open and close to grab or toss foods

Saucepan
round deep metal pan with a handle and a lid, used on a stovetop

Skewers
long, thin, pointed kitchen tools that hold foods together for cooking or eating

Skillet
round, shallow metal pan with a handle, used on a stovetop

Spatula
flat tool used to mix ingredients or scrape the side of a bowl

Spreader
tool used to put a thin layer of a soft food onto another food

Stockpot
round deep metal pot used for making larger amounts of food, used on the stovetop

Tube pan
a deep baking pan with a hole in the center to make cakes or breads

Turner
flat tool used to flip foods from one side to the other or to remove foods from a pan

Vegetable peeler
tool that separates the peel or skin of a fruit or vegetable from its flesh

Whisk
tool made of looped metal wires used to add air into a mixture by beating it rapidly

TECHNIQUE GLOSSARY

Beat
stir very quickly to help add air to a mixture

Blend
mix together, often in a blender

Boil
heat until small bubbles form on the top of a liquid

Chop
cut into small pieces

Dice
cut into very small pieces

Dissolve
incorporate a solid into a liquid by melting or stirring

Drain
remove liquid by pouring it off or placing it in a colander

Garnish
decorate

Grated
cut into small thin strips. To grate foods, you rub them against a grater—a flat metal kitchen tool covered with tiny blades and holes.

Knead
mix dough in a way to work the glutens (a type of protein found in flour). To knead dough, you flatten the dough with the heel of your hand, fold the dough in half, and press down again. Sprinkle your work surface with flour to keep the dough from sticking.

Mash
mush a soft food into a lumpy mixture

Melt
heat a food to turn it from solid to liquid

Mince
cut into the finest, smallest pieces

Peel
take off the outer covering (skin, rind, etc.) of a fruit or vegetable

Preheat
turn the oven on ahead of time so it reaches the correct temperature when you are ready to begin baking

Puree
blend a food until it is smooth

Slice
cut into thin pieces with a knife

Spread
put a thin layer of a soft food onto another food

Thaw
bring frozen food to room temperature

Toss
mix by lifting the ingredients in an up and down motion

"To Taste"
to your liking. Recipes often leave the amount of seasoning ingredients up to the cook, so you can add more or less, depending on what you like.

READ MORE

Dunnington, Rose. *Bake It Up!: Desserts, Breads, Entire Meals & More.* New York: Lark Books, 2006.

Greenwald, Michelle. *The Magical Melting Pot: America's Leading Chefs Share Childhood Memories and Favorite Foods.* Calif.: Cherry Press, 2003.

Hall, Dede. *The Starving Students' Vegetarian Cookbook.* New York: Warner Books, 2001.

Mills, Kevin, and Nancy Mills. *Help! My Apartment Has a Kitchen: 100+ Great Recipes with Foolproof Instructions.* Boston: Houghton Mifflin, 2006.

Stern, Sam. *Get Cooking.* Cambridge, Mass.: Candlewick Press, 2007.

INTERNET SITES

Use FactHound to find Internet sites related to this book. All of the sites on FactHound have been researched by our staff.

Here's all you do:
Visit *www.facthound.com*
Type in this code: 9780756544089

ACKNOWLEDGEMENTS

Many thanks to friends and family members who sampled my creations and shared recipe advice. I am grateful to Paula Meachen, Patricia Rau, Denise Genest, and the Tuesday morning writers. Additional thanks to the teens of my neighborhood who e-mailed me lists of their favorite foods. An extra nod to Chris, Charlie, and Allison, who ate and drank the good and the bad and never held back their honest opinions.

Dana Meachen Rau

INDEX

ABOUT THE AUTHOR

Dana Meachen Rau

Dana Meachen Rau is the author of more than 250 books for children, from preschoolers to teens. She loves baking cookies, shopping at local farms, and growing tomatoes and basil in her backyard garden. Her favorite food by far is chocolate. Even in summer, she usually enjoys a steaming cup of hot cocoa every day.